Tracts

For Ian

" The next street takes him
no closer to the station —
as he walks for the train."

Dave

— Feb 96 —

Tracts

Dave Ward

HEADLAND

First published 1996 by
Headland Publications
38 York Avenue, West Kirby
Wirral, Merseyside L48 3JF

Copyright © Dave Ward 1996

ISBN: 0 903074 90 7

A full C.I.P. record for this book
is available from the British Library.

Headland Publications acknowledges
the financial assistance of North West Arts Board

tract. n. A region or expanse
of indefinite extent & shape;
(Anat.) the part of the body
containing & connected with some
organ or performing some function;
a short treatise esp. one on
a religious subject printed for
gratis distribution.

Oxford English Dictionary

Acknowledgements:
Some of these poems first appeared in the following magazines:
*Blue Cage, Brando's Hat, Dream, The Echo Room, Foolscap,
Frogmore Papers, Hybrid, Issue One, Kindred Spirit* (U.S.A.),
Maryland Poetry Review (U.S.A.), *Memes, New Moon, Oasis,
Odyssey, The Pearl* (U.S.A.), *Poetry Nottingham, Poetry
Review, Poetry Wales, Psychopoetica, Scratch, Slow Dancer,
Something For Nothing, Staple, Stride, Takahe* (Aotearoa),
Verbal, Z Magazine; the anthologies *All In The Family* (Oxford
University Press), *Can You Hear: Poems For Oxfam* (Pan Piper);
and in the pamphlets *Braille* (Jonathon Press), *Stereo Soundtrack*
(Stride), *Tree* (Spike), *Uncle Strange* (Moonshine Press); and
broadcast on BBC School Radio and BBC Radio Merseyside.
"Each of the Bottles" also appears in *Candy and Jazzz* (Oxford
University Press).

Cover Art: *The Long Man of Wilmington*
at Windover Hill, Sussex. Batik by Brian Ward.
Back Cover Photograph: Rebecca Mothersole.

It is morning.
The ghost dancers wait in silence.
They take their shapes, take their places.
Gathering motes of colour, flecks of dust.
They gather substance.
                    Until.
One has the shape of a bird.
                    She sings.

The birdsong hobbles and pecks, rooting out
    warnings, rooting out barbed wire and
        diesel, rooting out the sound
            of dying flowers
                dying forests
            a dying planet.

She shapes them into a song, twisted
    with the mist, with the shiver
        of daybreak.

    A baby wakes and listens,
        lies still,
        welling shadows
        to imitate
        the birdsong's breathless tapestry.

    In an aching bed
the mother turns and holds her breast.
        She cannot hear
                the bird.
        She says the baby
                screams.

Each of the bottles is filled with water.
This is important to remember.
They may bear different names on the labels.
They may appear to be different colours.
But each of the bottles is filled with water.

They stand in a line on a stall
in the far corner of the market.

The first woman comes,
and buys one of the bottles.
She thinks the bottle contains wine.
She takes it home to drink with her husband.
They end the night tipsy with ecstasy, falling
into each other's arms.

The second woman comes,
and buys the second bottle.
She thinks the bottle contains perfume.
She takes it home and sprinkles it
on her arms and on her neck.
She smiles at the men who smile at her,
thinking they can smell the scent
that she cannot smell.

The third woman comes,
and buys the third bottle.
She thinks the bottle contains medicine.
She takes it home and gives a spoonful
to each of her sick children.
The next day their eyes are laughing
as they sing and play in the street.

The fourth woman comes,
and asks for water.
The stall-keeper shrugs and points at the labels.
The woman unscrews the largest bottle, the one
with the water dyed the most exotic colour,
the one with the highest price on the label.

"I'll take this one," she says, and stands
where she is and drinks every drop.
The stall-keeper, brazen-faced, still asks
for his money.
The woman bends down and picks up
a stone.
"Here is a loaf of bread," she says.

He opens the box.
    It is empty but
    he hears the clatter of pale wings.

He reaches into the box.
    It is empty but
    he feels the flutter of
    timid feathers. The frightened heart
    of a trapped bird.

He opens the window.
    Leans out over the sill,
    rattling the lid of
    the empty box
    with a flapping motion
    of his wrists.

        The box
    hangs open as he falls,
    and he hears the call
    of the grateful bird
    as it finds freedom in the wind.
    And as he glides
    towards the ground,
    he opens his mouth
        and sings.

Under towering storm clouds
two boys fight.

Dull rain plasters lank hair to their faces.
Strike and sway.
Smack and weave.

They dream they are soldiers
fighting for country,
fighting for causes,
fighting for sweethearts they haven't discovered.

The war goes on.
Not quite over.
Not quite begun.

And they laugh as they scream as they fight.

The pale sun hugs them
as they hug each other,
clutch each other,
drag each other down.

Tasting the sweetness of their own sweat.
Tasting the ground.

A ladder to nowhere
   where the rainbow ends,
  here in the
   broken playground.
Smashed glass
litters the tarmac
glinting sharp as pain.

   An echo space
   hung
   in this stone circle
   of towerblocks
  here where the lone dogs hunt
    and snarl.

But in the playground's singing
    ring
  between misshapen metal frames
  a pair of razzle-tousled girls
   pick the burning
   yellow flowers.

The boy sits on the shadow of
                the midday wall.
    As he eats from a sticky bag
        his grin slinks sideways,
            mouthing the slogans
                    scrawled
        above the chip shop door.
    The lopsided lettering
    recites the names
    of all the drugs
                the kids have
                heard of.
The boy chews slowly. Leans lazily.
        Learns the names
                    as
            the high sun
                    hangs.

Needle.
	Need.
			Need all.
	Sky-rise
		high line.
						All
						fall
					down.

		The walls alive
		with graffiti eyes.

		The windows blind
		only see inside.

		Litter in the stairwell.
		Piss in the lift.

		Empty sockets seep
		bad water.

	Nothing
	can fix
		this.

		No way out
		but up.

						All
						fall
					down.

The gates of the church are locked -
        but on the steps
        a boy in a zip black combat jacket
        plays pitch and toss
                with one lost penny -

as in the mist a wreath
        of bright red poppies glows,
        leant against the memorial
                        to names
        he's never read.

Two girls march
                their morris steps
                in the fallen leaves.

No music but
                the dusk's shy birdsong
        and the beat of plimsolled feet.

As the girls keep count
their grey eyes meet
                the colour of sky
                that rises
                        high beyond
                the clouds that cluster
        round the back-chat end
                of the street.

TUNNEL VISION

on this suburban station
where the silence
never answers back

an illiterate spraycan
hisses hate
in a canister of gas

the NF slogan capitals
slide as bold as cowardice
across the face
of the sign that reads
LIMITED HEADROOM

all the old
junk eyes
wait down here

       here
       where
       the elevators only travel
             down

in the subway
      under
  the subway

    even the buskers are dumb

      he watches
      this city
           destroying itself
           rebuilding itself
    again
    &
    again
      in the prism
          of
        each polluted
        teardrop

muffled silhouettes hover
                across frosty ground

outside the dull doorway
  high pitched voices
      shimmer
      frail as
  dead leaves trodden
      underfoot

                        above the subway
                        dark shapes roar

in the morning
it's all rough gossip
and dolequeue rumours

(under the lampost - he hit her/she screamed)

           he ran

he knows
the city like
        braille
                fathoms weather
                through
                the patterns
                of brick
                        dust

his arms
    are scarred
    a useless map
            of
            every dead end
                    street

chance conversations
seep into his veins
                lost headlines
                burnt letters
                whispered greetings
                echoing back
                along the wires

voices in the morning
that have been all night drinking
scour like broken milk bottles
out along the landings

babies wake like radios
and neighbours start complaining
as young mothers struggle to forget
their one night spent forgetting

they writhe
the rhythm of fishes
swimming together upstream

slippery bodies meshed
in a net of laughter

here is the answer
the willing
the needing

break through to the stillness
the whispering
    feeling

here
caught in the flow of the water
dreaming
        here

what stirs in the dream kitchen?

an owl flaps
in the bread bin

a spoonful of tears
sparkles in the sieve

time trickles
slow as sand
from the herb jars

a heart beats
inside the fridge

where is the cook?
is she sleeping?
at the bottom of the garden
on the compost heap
where snails drawl their
silver pathways
across her swollen legs

the stooping woman
carries a basket of stones
around the shopping precinct

people watch her
weighted down with her load

one day
a young girl
puzzled but willing
offers to carry it for her

as soon as she takes it
she feels the dull pain
pull across her shoulders
and when she looks up
the stoopiong woman has gone

her body fades
as she passes each tree
she seems to grow fainter
until
at the end of the street
she is not there
and as the leaves drift down
she was never there
at all

The door opens.
The man is dressed in carpet slippers.
He smiles, unconvincingly.

The door closes.

We wait.

The door opens again.
The man is dressed in running shoes.
He jogs on the spot, breathlessly.

The door closes.

We wait.

The door opens again.
The man is dressed in an apron.
He throws cups and dishes at us, viciously.

We wait for the door to close.

It stays open.

We gather up armfuls of shattered crockery,
walk inside and close the door.

There is a knock at the door.

We drop the crockery.

And open the door.

A man stands outside.
He is dressed in a hatchet and a bloodstained knife.
He smiles, convincingly.

The silver ring slides from her finger.
The curtains sway gently: a warm breeze.
A man is walking towards the house,
his face in shadow under
the wide brim of his hat.

She hears the knock at the door.
She pauses.
Long fingers playing with the ring.

He knocks again and thinks he hears her
laughing.   The flowers around her porch
are faded.

Upstairs, she sits in silence. The clock
on the mantelpiece has stopped. Its face
dull with dust. The knocking at the door
continues, louder. She crosses the room,
                                    slowly,
leaving the ring lying on the table.

The front door opens. He sees
a small girl in a print dress. She
sees a young boy clutching a
fistful of withered flowers.

In the room, the clock ticks. Laughter.

She stands alone on the stone bridge
        above the skimming stream.

She drops flowers into the water
                        one by one.
                Each flower a wish.
                Each flower a prayer.
The flowers are dark. They float
                        away.
                                She
        does not watch.

                Brooding clouds huddle above
                                the hills.
                In the fields a haggle of rooks,
                their eyes harsh
                                as the storm.

On the bridge she scatters the last of the petals
into the scudding wind. She wears a brooch
the shape of the moon.
                Her long fingers
                        caress it
                as she runs.

He opens the door behind the velvet curtain.
A small turret room.
Sunlight squints through the high window.
The woman is seated on a white stool.
On the low round table
in front of her,
a game of chess.
Beside the table, a white bowl.
The bowl is filled with oranges.

She combs long fingers through her
black flowing hair and reaches out
to move the white queen.
She never looks
at the man.

He takes one orange from the bowl,
and splits it with his knife.

She opens a window
          inside herself
and sits to watch
the city dance.

          The stuttering man
          still worrying people for money
          in front of the cathedral
          that looms as huge
                    as loneliness
                    behind him.

          A woman in a fur coat,
          her face caked with make-up,
          her body bleeding jewelry,
          hailing the taxi-cabs
                    that will not stop.
          They know she never
                    pays them.

          The singing girl who shuffles
                    round the nervous staircase.
          The walls are brown and
                    she smiles pink lipstick.
          One of her fingers
                    is missing.

Darkness dreams
          into her glass
          as she sips
                    the stillness
          cradled in her hands.

She stands in the doorway,
unsure of herself.

In the pale silence
she wears
a white dress.

Wandering wasteground
gathering wild flowers
to take back to her room
where she spends all day
watching them
wither and fade.

Three jesters on the edge of time.

One dreams he is
locked in a prison cell,
with the sound of looting
dinning on
deep inside his ear drums.

One dreams he sits
in a painted room
where no-one comes and
no-one goes except
for those who hang the moon.

One dreams he is not
dreaming, but the other
two dream of him.
In one dream
he is the gaoler, twisting
                    the dreaded key.
In the next
he is the artist
whose stars spin still
across the walls
                    of the painted room.

When the jesters wake, they smile,
for each one thinks
                he knows
                who the other two think
                he is.

Under stark arches, she watches the water.
Through the wounds where grey bullets
                    of rain break through
she sees a city below the surface,
        minarets and balconies, spiralling fountains
        line wide sweeping boulevards
        where sumptuous trees bow heavy with fruit.

But the faces of the people
are charts creased with sadness as
they shuffle slow as blindness
between the glowing flowers.

                    Up above her head, she hears
                    the dull trains rattle
                    and behind her
                    the raw-throated song
                    of the chains
                    that clatter dankly
                    on the derelict wharf.

Then she turns as she hears
laughter floating gently, and voices
clear as crystal
                    singing to the wind
                    and she sees
the empty windows
the silent unhinged doorways
alive with dancing masks,
                    a carnival
                            of porpoises
                    and tall proud whales
                                    calling.

A flower.

         It grows beside the barbed wire
         and the slack pools thick with
         brick dust.

            It grows
            with the din of clanking trains,
            with the clatter of the factory
            continuously.
                   It grows
            with the smell
            of chemicals that smell
            of the smell of powdered bones.

It grows
and dies
and grows again,
watching while the landscape shifts,
                roads and dwellings
                wheel and drift,
                daughters of mothers'
                daughters come and love
                and go.

It grows.

tell me the colour
of time

draw me a map
of the night

string my fingers
with strands of the sky

and I will bring you
a bowl full of light

where do dreams go?

they are trapped by bare branches
of trees that have been stripped
of yellowing leaves

float like lost balloons
bouncing and beckoning through
the gullies and gutters of deserted streets

fumble wondering from the warmth
of old sleeping bags
to peer at their reflections in strangers' mirrors

me? - I keep a fistful
stuffed inside my pockets
and carry them with me
to give to you

across worlds
my mouth becomes
your mouth

each touch
a question
and every answer
a touch

our bodies know
so many meanings
when we say
    we love

and prove together
over and over
this one small word
is not enough

when the air is filled
with turning birds
let us join hands
and dance

as the sun draws blood
above grey roofs
our tongues converse
in silence

as the cusp of the moon
cuts the sky like a knife
these bodies exchange
sweet milk

not a bird
but the shadow of a bird
darted across the garden

not a child
but the echo of far-off laughter
tumbled between the overgrown walls

not a flower
but a wind-blown seed
whispered above the moist warm soil

not a dream
but a friend for all reasons
trod the uneven pathway
to knock at my door

In this hall!
           of mirrors
           we do not
    speak.
           Only watch
                     each other
                     's distorted images
           follow
                     each other
           and never touch.
Even
       when we turn a corner
       and meet
                 our own reflections
                 we do not recognise
       who we are.

S

He walks for the train. The streets are snagged with leaves, with tears. He sees faces behind gauze curtains. He recognises them as his children, but they do not smile, do not wave, as he walks for the train. He recalls their births, each long night, each sunrise. A sickle moon. A cobweb cough. The mother moan, the gasp. The twilight clutching dawn. Warm smell of earth blood clogging nostrils.

The next street takes him no closer to the station as he walks for the train. He lengthens his stride, yet walks no faster. On the corner he sees his daughter. She smiles at him, waves, but he does not answer. Tightlipped. He thinks she is his mother. He cannot remember his own birthing, their own pain. The train is late. He is late for the train.

He hears it in the distance. Its rhythm beats a heart, a pulse of ecstacy. He has ridden this train before, before, each wide-eyed morning. At the carriage windows he knows he will see: his wife, old lovers, his mother's mother. But today the train is far away. As he turns the corner, sees a boy watching him with eyes that are his own, each new street leads him on, further from the station.

Chill room. The child with the shaven head sits at a twisted desk. One in a line, in a line of lines. An empty classroom, hung with dust, the windows smashed. Ashes in the fireplace. The floor is strewn with pages torn from withered books.

Above the teacher's desk a portrait watches. A woman in a grey dress. He knows it is his mother. She watches the room, the faded maps on the walls, the charts and tables, the chanting figures. Her boy is all alone.

But at the desk, he plays. Plays with the bright toys he has brought from his nursery. A sailor doll, a scarlet train. He is laughing.

Outside in the brick yard, filled with sandpits and climbing frames, bats and balls and hopscotch chalks, the children snarl and bite, scream abuse, shrill mockingly; spit and fight.

A man wears a coat of eagle feathers. He walks alone. The street shadows lengthen, follow. Cornershops close their doors. Weather-worn hoardings leer and beckon. Behind the terraced houses which squat and watch, rats claw and scurry as they sense his coming. Children gawp wide-eyed and dare each other to chase after and steal one of his plumes.

The man walks into a cafe. The hiss of the tea-urn, the clatter of knives. The windows are steamed with damp conversation. The customers are wrapped in newspapers and dreams. They busy themselves with cold pies and coffee, not daring to look at the man, even though his coat of eagle feathers fills them with fascination, with envy, with loathing.

He drinks from a chipped cup, slowly, gazes wistfully about the room. As he hunches his shoulders, as he crooks his arm, feathers fall from the coat. A trail of lost feathers leads back across the tiled floor, out into the street.

A girl comes in. She wears electric lipstick and lopsided earrings. She clutches a fistful of eagle feathers. She stares about the room as if she is looking for someone, but seems not to see the man wearing the coat.

Disappointed, she sits in a corner seat, watching the street, counting the feathers that she spreads on the table, as if she is waiting for someone to arrive.

From the shadows walk three figures: an old man, a young woman and a child. Their fingers touch as they lead each other, across a hillside strewn with ashes, across a hillside where white flowers burn. They lead each other towards the river which curves between dark fields. Wading out into the water, the man, the woman and the laughing child kiss each other in turn.

Dawn mist lifts in silver birdsong as they climb glistening onto the opposite bank, and their gaze rises up to the distant mountains, disappearing into cloud. Their limbs reach out, pointing, beckoning; reckoning every step of their jouney. Silhouetted by the rising sun they stand like trees, stretching towards the shimmering sky.

Feel the keening,
             the dream and drift.
Slow clouds collide, unravel, turn.
In fields stocked with thunder
             the long sun grows,
             and voices
sing thistledown,
             gathering.

Her body pocked
             by the burn of lost comets,
             ghost planets turn in her eyes.
She sits unmoving, earth-locked, time-bound,
             reading the pulsar beats
             pounding her skull.
At the frontiers of dusk she
                  charts the stars,
             counting eternities on the end
                  of chewed nails.

Her face opens. In this
              wound dark
                    moths erupt.
             And livid creatures,
             pale as frost,
             each one screaming,
                   tearing,
                   speaking,
in thin sinews
stretched
       and hung
between
barbed branches.

Country music plays along
the old truck trails.

                 She rides
                 away
                 from the wailing.

White line drives
           in headlamp eyes.

It's a wildcat night.
She's leaving.

Road-dancing,
                    the cars, they
                    spin and turn
                    stretch and
                                spit,
                    chasing dark suns
                                stolen moons
                    they fly.

On the radio, voices jabber, scream and mix.
The whine of time, a cobweb stretched, a
wire mesh. The machines do not listen, dumb
as they speed.

                    The journey is
                    the journey
                    never ends.

The sun deceives.
                    It is not
                    a demon dancer. It is not
                    a silent watcher. It is
                    not a god.

            But we breathe it
                    we taste it
                    we lie with it naked
                                as sated lovers.

                    And we fear
                    the lizard shadows
                    of its last eclipse.

RADIO TIMES

Those were radio times,
When rock'n'roll lines rang out in every bedroom.

We lived radio lives,
We'd twist and we'd jive
        to the backbeat of every station.

The electricity surged
Through the rhythm we heard
        crackling across the airways.

Our street corner games
Were never quite the same:
        shuffling dancesteps under the stairways.

Sweet Polly Smith,
Her starlit kiss writhed a rhapsody down the back entry.

Total strangers' voices
Became our closest friends,
Jammed in a room on a hot afternoon,
        counting down the latest Top Twenty.

We turned on to Hendrix
At the same time as sex,
        and made love to Ginger Baker's drum solos,

With the dial turned around
To maximum sound in the front room
        without any clothes on.

The raw Rolling Stones
Broke into every home,
Just where every daughter's mother wouldn't want them.

But when Kennedy died
The music nationwide was sad and sombre and solomn.

Those were radio times
Laced with overflowing rhyme
As we drank sweet wine by the river.

Those were radio times,
We couldn't dream what we would find -
As if each crazy summer night would last forever....

I USED TO BE YOUNG

She waves the day away
While she watches children play
From behind the misty curtains of the home.

Though they sometimes grin and greet her,
Their voices never reach her:
Trapped behind the tall black railings, she waits alone.

"I used to be young," her mouth shapes the words.
"I used to be young," though nobody hears.
"I used to be young, and what did I do? -
Spent the day playing, the same as all you."

Her memory follows them down to the water,
Watches the surface reflections shiver
Like lost recollections, the ripples quiver -
As a child drops a stone, it sinks and it's gone,
But the waves that it makes travel on and on.

She thinks life begins like a pebble in a pond:
"I may be old now, but I used to be young."
As she waves one more wave at the end of the day;
"The ripples keep spreading all through our lives,"
One more wave closer to the other side.

She is making a cake.

She makes it with cherries, sultanas and raisins.
She makes it with salt,
with flour and with tears.

Takes them and weighs them
on uneven scales
that have always been tilted against her.

She weighs the moments,
the laughter,
the pain.

She weighs up the waiting,
the ploys,
and the games.

Her children ask if they can scrape the bowl.
With a great wooden spoon
they savour the smiles,
lick at the loving,
the sweet golden lies.

She bakes the smooth mixture
in an oven of gas,
pacing the kitchen
as she wills it to rise.

Then her children come straggling
in from their play
to cut thick heavy slices,
still steaming and warm
which they chew in dumb silence
and leave her just one lonely crumb.

She stitches a patchwork quilt.
Nimble fingers pick the moments,
    pluck and gather squares
    of silence
    that tumble warmly round her knees.

The vase in the window
filled with sharp teazles.

The drawers in the cabinet
packed with reels of bright thread.

    She sings and sews, not
    listening to the news
    that seeps like a rumour
    from the old radio.

While on the shelf
above the whispering fire
    the dark clock ticks,
        a heartbeat.

they rode like ragged birds
over the horizon
flapping a ramshackle collection
of bags and pans

scarecrow silhouettes
drained of colour
in shapeless caps and proud
patched coats
turned against the weather

their bivouac shelters perched
under the railway's stern embankment
grey canvas sheeting
huddled
against the straggling woodland
where fields and meadow met

their bicycles
tall metal stallions
that moved in silent convoy
along slow gravel roadways
spare parts sewn and knitted
into their heavy frames

in the middle of the street
in the middle of town
at midnight
he is scraping
a piece of chewing gum
from the tarmac

he moves methodically
stooped in the glare -
staring back at the headlamps
of swooping cars

picking up paper
picking up fagends

he seaches the gutter
numb fingers scrabbling
at the dead leaves & sweet wrappers

looks up at his audience
shuffling in the doorway
of the hamburger cafe

"i've come to
clean up your town"
he says

he wore
a gawky mac
in the rain
by the roadside

clumsy hands clutching
one battered football

his eyes blinking
cracked headlamps
peering at the lorries

a lost boy's voice
trapped deep
in his dad's
hand-down jacket

flapping at the traffic
"stop all the cars
stop all the cars
somebody come
& play football with me"

The sleeping man wakes. Outside his window, the jigsaw of streets. Inside his head, the map is smudged. The clouds in his eyes drift and blur.

*

A forest. The voice follows him. He no longer listens to the words. They are lost. Only the tune, a sinew of silver.

Underneath dark bushes, the lurid flowers dream.

*

A frozen garden. Here the gaunt branches scream. Here a crystal silence hangs in the dead fruit's withered shell.

*

Beyond silence, a pale light. The echo of beginning. The pulse of conception. The aching wind. The stillness. This is journey beyond reason. Into the region where the tranquil rhythms travel without time.

*

These are connections. White stars blaze in a journey of darkness. Each moment a memory, a time alone, a touchstone of discovery.

*

Each last supper tastes the same. A sad birthday party. The one meal laid in your honour that you can never share, as brothers, sisters, distant cousins gather. The flesh connection, the broken chain, as they dance a drab room sharing whispers and suffering, stuttering laughter, and the sweet cup of guilt that gags on the pain.

This your house, this your room, where they gather without you and speak only about you without ever mentioning your name.

You watch a last time before leaving. Close the door as quietly as you did every day, and tiptoe away, not wanting to disturb their helpless grieving. For them, the journey has ended. For you, the journey has only begun.

SIX RITUALS

I

Ritual of
  the moon of blood.
        Swimming low
          she drinks
          dark fields,
      the slack water lapping;
   purged, she climbs high
            again
       linking with her
            silent sister,
    to dance
    this urgent secrecy,
    a season's scarlet
         lunacy:
         treachery's slow
            flood.

II

     Ritual of silence,
           of knives and ashes.
           Of leaden sky.
      Across burnt fields the
             April Fool
             lugs black eggs
               in her ragged apron.
     The dead tree waits
           with outstretched arms
          as twelve sisters
      follow her
      baring the nails.

III

Ritual of
    the sleeping death.
    The weeping maze, we enter,
    trusting in our fear;
  we cling to threads, a web
    of dreaming.

  The relics of each sleeping,
talisman and portent,
    greet us as we stumble
into dumb awakening.

        The screaming mirror.
        The lidded eyes.
      The lizard garden, the
      shedding skin.
      The broken moon,
    the sullen dawn.
      The bruised lips of
        remembering.

IV

Ritual of the love-struck fool,
                    moon-eyed
                and dancing
            where there is
                    no tune
                        only
        a rhythm
        of hidden whispers,
        the hint of an eyelid,
        and the mesh of fingers.

The barbed root,
the seeding tree,
                he is lost and
                will follow
        until he loses all
            he has
                    never found.

V

Ritual of leaving,
 the grieving leaf,
 the shedding
  of flesh.
    In this
    ritual of skin
  there are no prisoners.

The drugged kiss,
  the blood's eclipse.
  Sea fret and tamarisk.

Lust knots the rope,
  a tightening coil,
 in the cradle
    of the hollow groin.

VI

Ritual of the circles.

Circle of blood.
Circle of stone.
Circle of earth.
Circle of moon.

The dancers do not know
they dance
as the circles turn
within them,
yet their limbs step and quicken
to the rhythm's pulse
as each circle turns
them round.

Circle of earth.
Circle of moon.
Circle of blood.
Circle of stone.

Circle of circles.
The mother moan.
The sister rib.
The daughter wound.

under the rain
reflections

tarmac river
drains

railings frail
against the waves

grey questions
break unanswered

the circus of dreams
is not always what it seems
stealing between dead hedgerows
to frozen memories of meadows

where beside the moonlit water
the madonna and her daughter
watch the caravans roll by
in unsung silence

but in the distant city streets
a boy she never meets
is still dancing to the drumbeat
in the circus of his dreams

we are the mirror people
you cannot see us
we live in the diseased places
of the cities you deserted

sleep in the shuffling shadows
on the stairways
of the crumbling towerblocks
that used to be your homes

you will never find us
as we eat into your blindness
and dance in the sullen emptiness
that grows between your eyes

cool wind

one blackbird sings
on the twisted rafters
of the wrecked maisonettes

the children
are lighting bonfires

their faces masks
of emptiness
marked with grime
& rain

circling & cowering
a baptism of stone

the bone men chant
in broken voices
up & down
the drizzling street

trailing burst balloons
& banners of rags

no-one can hear what
they're saying

but from the shadows
of watching doorways
the waiting women
throw back their words

the old houses rot

men build a high fence round them

to stop other men from getting in
to take the metal and the wood

the high fence blows down
the men build a new one

the new fence grows holes
for children to crawl through

the holes grow still bigger
till the wood and the metal
from the old rotting houses
creeps away in the night

they build a new fence
of new wood and new metal
so strong and so shining
it will never fall down

the children climb over
and hide in the houses
their young voices echo
with memories and hope

then the wind blows again
and flames lick through the rafters

and one night behind the high fence
built of metal and strong timber
the old rotting houses
crack and slither to the ground

we dance
we dance
the demon dance
through sour demented rain

poison blooms
a fever trance

jealousy breeds
dumb romance

one drum beats back
the emptiness
in the house of the insane

the dread gods wait
un-named
under these streets of blood & dust

we will not raise them
with our dumb rituals
of carnival lust

this is a season of loneliness
when each one of us
must work out a destiny

but without our gods & demons
our dancers & our dreaming
we are lost
in this dark season
without purpose
without reason

we speak
in lost tongues
dragged from the echoes
of forgotten wells

no longer visited
by singing processions
carrying flower pictures
thumb-pressed in damp clay

these rough voices
clutch at the edge
of dark silence
coughing bile & disease
to the dull drumbeat's thrum

when the dull dawn's eye opens
to the stark white of blindness
as the sky explodes -
where will we go to?

when the high priests of silence
offer up the last rites
for the world they tore open
while they stole from its gods

at the crack of the atom
will the last dust of earth
blow endlessly nowhere -
or is this the rebirth
we sought for so long?

the voices
the shadows
the dreams
all reform

we dance without bodies
we sing without tongues

it is not
his risen body
we worship

but the dead flesh
nailed
where we left it

high on that cross
of silent wood

like a dumb mute
listening helplessly
to the mutterings & cursings
the taking of his name
in vain
he mistook for love & brotherhood
as the watchful seasons turned

but now he knows
it is death
we praise
in chants that crawl
from tongues of slime

death to any
that would be saviour

death to brother
death to sister

death to every
fowl & beast
that dance alive
through sky & land

from birth with every breath
we take
we shape
our own death
with relentless hands

where do the bones grow?
under the streets
under the pavements
the city's a garden
the bones are the seed
we are the flowers
dancing & burning
turning through subways
& spiralling liftshafts
out to the rooftops
singing
exploding
we reach for the sun

i have something
i want to say to you

take this husk
i hold in my hand

don't lose it
it's all there is left

before the wind blows it
imagine

this was once
seed
was grain
was life
was a field of weaving
vivid yellow with laughter

open your hand now
see
the wind catches the husk &
carries it away

soon to be dust
but dust never dies

is the bed
of the new soil

breathing

new earth

TREE

tree
was here before me

tree
will still be here
when I have gone

tree
gathers life
from the sun

sun
was here before me

sun
will still be here
when I have gone

tree
drinks life
from the rain

rain
was here before me

rain
will still be here
when I have gone

tree
roots life
from the earth

earth
was here before me

earth
will still be here
when I have gone

tree
spreads life
by the wind

wind
was here before me

wind
will still be here
when I have gone

I am only here
a short time

I call on sun: teach me
I call on rain: teach me
I call on earth: teach me
I call on wind: teach me
teach me
to use my short time well

beside this tree
when I have gone
sun will measure
the shadow of my short time here
shed like rain
across the earth

while in the wind
my memory sings

teach me
to use my short time well
soon
I will be gone

THE GREEN MAN DANCES

The Green Man dances in the wood
By withered nettles where the oaks once stood
The Green Man dances in the wood
But the trees scream murder
As we burn them down

The Green Man has danced out under the stars
Under changing skies for a million years
Silver in the morning and the coal black night
Waking again for the last long fight

The Green Man dances in the wood
By broken glass where the tall cedar stood
The Green Man dances in the wood
But the trees wail murder
As we axe them down

Now the Green Man grieves by the poisoned stream
Weeping bitter scalding tears
The badger, the otter and the hare lie dead
Dark rooks drift in circles as the sky turns red

The Green Man dances in the wood
By barbed wire fences where the elm once stood
The Green Man dances in the wood
But the trees weep murder
As we hack them down

The Green Man danced wherever he chose
Before forests were stolen and fields enclosed
The Green Man danced before winding lanes
Twisted into the madness of motorways

The Green Man dances in the wood
By dark choking shadows where the larches stood
The Green Man dances in the wood
But the trees whisper murder
As we rip them down

The hounds bay blindly where foxes used to run
But the hunt for the Green Man goes on and on
The ring of shrinking woodland tightens in a snare
As the Green Man tracks frantic as a frightened hare

The Green Man dances in the wood
By brackish water where the broad beech stood
The Green Man dances in the wood
But the trees breathe murder
As we smash them down

We'll catch him and beat him
And twist a jagged wreath
We'll whip him and scourge him
And nail him like a thief
To the highest branch
Of his last oak tree
With blackbird, dunnock, jackdaw and crow...
But when the Green Man dies,
We all die too.

the world is singing
let us sing

the world is spinning
let us spin

the world turns dreaming
let us turn dreams

let us not cry
for a dying world

for if we
sing and spin our dreams

this is not the end
this is only
the beginning